THE ILLUSTRATED
ENCYCLOPEDIA

VOLUME 1

A - B

Belitha Press

First published 1995 by
Macmillan Education Australia Pty Ltd

First published in the United Kingdom in 1995 by
 Belitha Press Limited
31 Newington Green, London N16 9PU

Cataloguing in print data available from the British Library.

ISBN 1 85561 520 7 (Vol 1)
ISBN 1 85561 529 0 (Set)

Consultant: Frances Warhurst
UK editor: Maria O'Neill
Project editor: Jo Higgins

Typeset by Polar Design
Printed in Hong Kong

Acknowledgements

The author and publishers are grateful to the following for permission to reproduce copyright material:

Cover: Horizon International

The Australian Ballet, p. 32 (top); Bureau of Meteorology, p. 7; Coo-ee Picture Library, pp. 4 (top), 13 (top), 14 (top), 16, 21 (bottom, centre & right), 29 (top left), 35 (bottom), 37, 38, 43, 47, 48, 53, 54, 58, 59, 63 (bottom); Civil Aviation Authority, p. 9 (top centre); CSIRO/Division of Entomology, p. 44 (left); W. Fagan, pp. 14 (bottom), 22, 29 (top right), 52 (right); Horizon International, pp. 41 (bottom), 42 (top); International Photographic Library, pp. 20, 21 (top & bottom left), 26 (bottom left), 27 (top left), 39, 41 (top); Gerard Lacy/A.N.T. Photo Library, p. 11; Mantis Wildlife Films, pp. 15, 42 (bottom), 63 (top); NASA, pp. 24, 25, 27 (insert); Northside Photographics, pp. 6, 13 (bottom), 18 (left), 23 (right), 28, 32 (bottom), 33, 44 (right), 52 (bottom left), 57 (left & bottom); The Photo Library, p. 63 (centre); QANTAS Australia, pp. 4, 5, 9 (right & bottom); Sporting Pics, p. 29 (top, centre & bottom); Stock Photos, pp. 23 (left), 31 (top), 45, 61; Norbert Wu/A.N.T. Photo Library, p. 18 (right); Carl Zeiss, p. 27 (bottom).

While every care has been taken to trace and acknowledge copyright the publishers tender their apologies for any accidental infringement where copyright has proved untraceable.

Illustrators

Sharyn Madder: 10, 11, 15, 20, 21, 39, 40, 41
Rhyll Plant: 16, 17, 18, 42, 43, 44, 52
John Fairbridge: 12, 22, 26, 27, 34, 35, 45, 46, 47, 53, 54, 55, 58, 59, 60, 61
Paul Konye: 4, 5, 6, 7, 8, 9, 13, 14, 28, 29, 32, 33, 36, 37, 38
Andrew Plant: 19, 23, 48, 51, 62, 64
Xiangyi Mo: 30, 56

HOW TO USE THIS BOOK

The Illustrated Encyclopedia has over 300 entries. The entries are arranged alphabetically. To find your topic, use the guide letters at the top of each page to check you have the right volume. The first letter of your topic will be highlighted.

TOPIC: ALLIGATOR

guide letter

A B C D E F G H I J K L M

Use the guide words printed in the top right-hand corner of each page to find your topic. The guide words list the entries on a double-page spread. They are listed alphabetically. Check the guide words to see if you need to go backwards or forwards.

guide word

ALLIGATOR

You can also use the index in Volume 9 to find your topic.

alligator
    Volume 1   **10 – 11**
    Volume 7   20

If you cannot find your topic in its alphabetical order in the encyclopedia, use the index.

crocodile
    see alligator
    see reptiles

TOPIC: CROCODILE

The index lists all the topics in alphabetical order. It tells you where you will find your topic.

More information on how to use the encyclopedia and the index can be found in Volume 9.

AEROPLANE

SEE ALSO • Airport • Jet engine • Transport

An aeroplane is a machine that can fly. Aeroplanes can carry a lot of passengers. They also carry cargo such as food or animals. Travelling by aeroplane is the fastest way to get from one place to another.

PARTS OF AN AEROPLANE

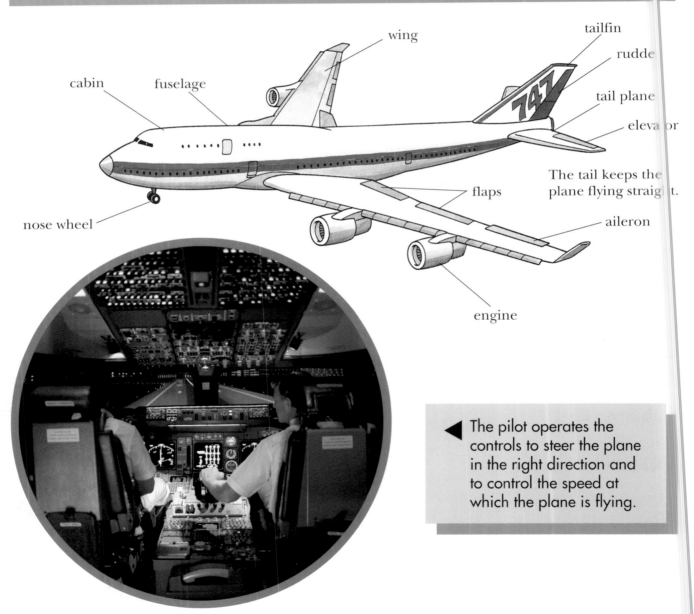

wing

tailfin

rudder

cabin

fuselage

tail plane

elevator

The tail keeps the plane flying straight.

flaps

aileron

nose wheel

engine

The pilot operates the controls to steer the plane in the right direction and to control the speed at which the plane is flying.

4

HISTORY

In 1903, Orville and Wilbur Wright made the first flight using a machine with an engine. The first aeroplanes were made of wood, wire and cloth.

HOW AN AEROPLANE FLIES

Four forces act on an aeroplane when it is flying.

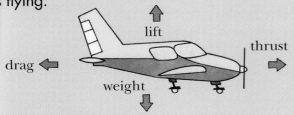

- Thrust is the force that moves an object forwards.
- Drag is air resistance that holds the plane back.
- Lift is an upward force that holds an aeroplane in the air.
- Weight is the force that pulls the aeroplane downwards.

Lift comes from an aeroplane's wings. The wings are a special shape called an aerofoil. The bottom of the wing is straight. The top of the wing is curved. Air has further to go over the top of the wing than under the wing. This produces a lifting pressure over the wings which supports the weight of the aeroplane.

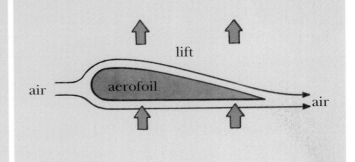

TAKE-OFF

An aeroplane travels faster and faster down the runway. The lift on the wings becomes greater and greater. When the lift equals the weight of the aeroplane, it rises into the air and flies. As long as the aeroplane is going fast enough, it will stay in the air.

AIR

SEE ALSO • Atmosphere • Earth • Gas • Pollution • Wind

Air is all around us. It is invisible. Air has no colour, smell or taste. Moving air is called wind.

 Animals and plants need air to live.

You can feel air when it moves. When air moves it presses against everything in its path. ▼

Air is a mixture of gases. Air contains nitrogen and oxygen. It also contains water vapour, dust and small amounts of other gases.

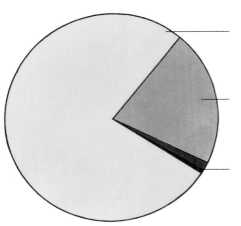

nitrogen
78 per cent

oxygen
21 per cent

other gases,
dust and water
vapour
1 per cent

AIR MAKES THINGS MOVE

Air pressure can force a drink through a straw. Air pressing down on the water pushes the water when you suck through a straw.

Air can turn windmills.

Air can move branches on a tree.

Air can blow sailboats across the water.

ATMOSPHERE

The layer of air around the Earth is called the atmosphere.
The atmosphere provides oxygen for all living things.

Earth ——————————

atmosphere ——————————

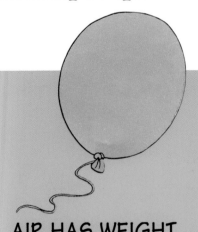

AIR HAS WEIGHT

If balloons are filled with a gas called helium, the balloon will float. Helium is lighter than air.

AIR SHOWS RESISTANCE TO MOVEMENT

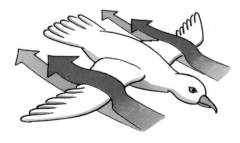

Air pushing against aeroplanes and birds keeps them flying.

Air resistance slows a parachute jumper's fall.

AIRPORT

SEE ALSO • Aeroplane • Helicopter • Radar • Transport

An airport is a place where aeroplanes take off and land. At large airports, many aeroplanes carrying passengers and goods arrive and leave every day. Other airports are smaller for smaller planes. Military airports have planes that belong to the army, navy or air force.

PARTS OF AN AIRPORT

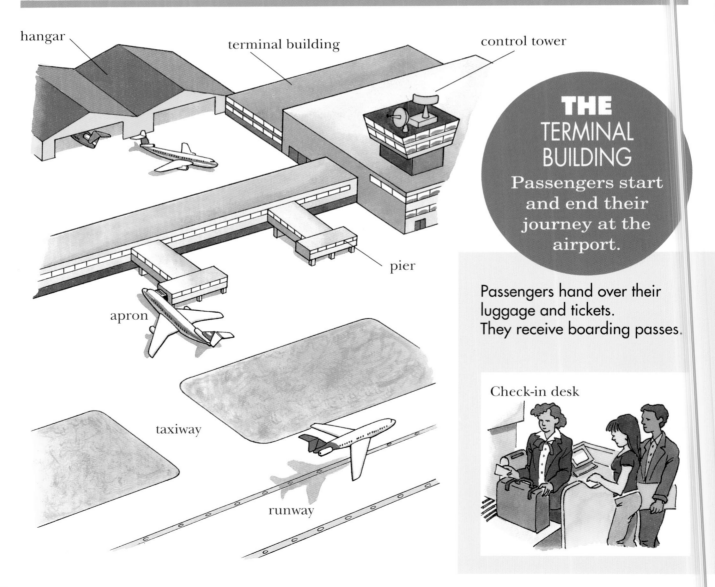

hangar

terminal building

control tower

pier

apron

taxiway

runway

THE TERMINAL BUILDING
Passengers start and end their journey at the airport.

Passengers hand over their luggage and tickets. They receive boarding passes.

Check-in desk

AIR TRAFFIC ▶ CONTROL

Air traffic controllers guide aeroplanes as they take off and land.

HANGARS ▼

Aeroplanes are stored and repaired in hangars.

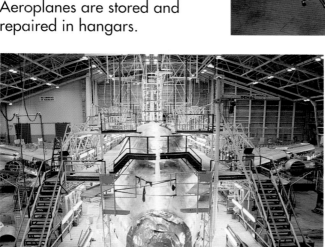

APRON ▶

Aeroplanes park on the apron. They are refuelled and loaded with cargo, luggage and passenger food.

TAXIWAY

Aeroplanes move along the taxiway between the apron, hangars and runway.

RUNWAYS

Aeroplanes take off and land on runways.

Passengers are checked to make sure they are not carrying anything dangerous.

Officials check passports. This helps them to keep a record of people leaving and entering a country.

Customs officials check passengers' baggage when they arrive in a country. They check for goods that are not allowed, such as drugs.

Security

Passport control

Customs

ALLIGATOR

SEE ALSO • Animal • Reptile

An alligator is a reptile.
The alligator is closely related to the crocodile.
Alligators can walk on land and swim in water.

PARTS OF AN ALLIGATOR

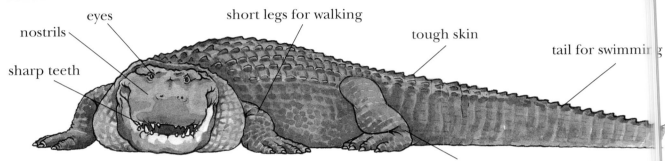

nostrils
eyes
short legs for walking
tough skin
tail for swimming
sharp teeth
legs held close to body for swimming

AMERICAN ALLIGATOR

Weight:
Male   200 to 250 kilograms
Female   80 kilograms

Length:
Male   5 metres
Female   2.5 metres

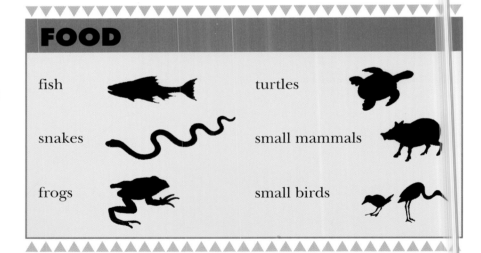

FOOD

fish
turtles
snakes
small mammals
frogs
small birds

KINDS OF ALLIGATORS

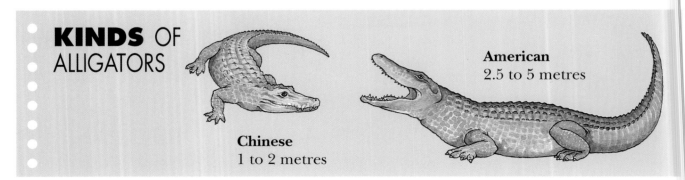

Chinese
1 to 2 metres

American
2.5 to 5 metres

P

INTERESTING FACT

Alligators and crocodiles live together in the swamps of Florida, USA.

An alligator's eyes and nose are on the top of its head. This is useful for when it is swimming.

WHERE ALLIGATORS LIVE

■ **North America**
South-eastern parts of USA
● **China**
Lower Yangtse River

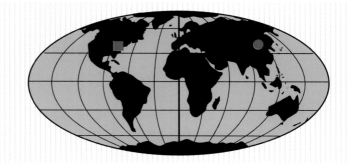

HOW ALLIGATORS LIVE

Alligators lay their eggs in nests made of grass and plants. The nests are 1 metre high and 2.5 metres wide.

20 to 60 eggs

ALLIGATORS AND CROCODILES

alligator

crocodile

- An alligator's fourth lower tooth fits into a pocket on its upper jaw; a crocodile's tooth is on the outside of its jaw.
- An alligator has a wider, blunter snout than a crocodile.
- Alligators are less aggressive and less active than crocodiles.

Alligators are about 20 centimetres long when they are born. Their mother looks after them for one year. Every year they grow about 30 centimetres until they reach their full-grown size at about eight years old.

Just born
20 centimetres

First year
50 centimetres

Second year
80 centimetres

Third year
110 centimetres

ALPHABET

SEE ALSO • Library • Name

An alphabet is a group of letters or symbols used in writing a language. Each symbol or letter represents a different sound. The letters can be arranged to form all the words in a language.

ROMAN ALPHABET

English is written using the 26 letters of the Roman alphabet. In English, some letters have more than one sound. Most other European languages use this alphabet, but some letters have different sounds. There are several alphabets used today.

Aa	Bb	Cc	Dd	Ee	Ff
Gg	Hh	Ii	Jj	Kk	Ll
Mm	Nn	Oo	Pp	Qq	Rr
Ss	Tt	Uu	Vv	Ww	Xx
Yy	Zz				

ALPHABETICAL ORDER

In alphabets, letters have a set order. Alphabetical order helps people to find things quickly.

CUNEIFORM ▲ WRITING

Thousands of years ago, people started to use symbols to represent sounds.

HOW EARLY PEOPLE COMMUNICATED

- When people first started writing, they drew a picture for each word.

- People then made up symbols to represent different sounds. They could write words by joining the symbols.

- This was the beginning of the alphabet.

ALUMINIUM

| SEE ALSO | • Metal • Mining • Recycling • Rocks |

Aluminium is a silvery white metal. It is light, strong and does not rust. Metals are found in the Earth's crust. Aluminium is the most common metal. It comes from bauxite which is found in rocks.

quarry

Bauxite is mined in quarries. Aluminium is separated from bauxite at a processing plant.

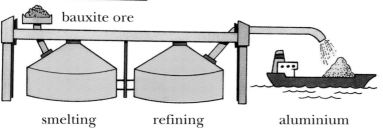
bauxite ore

smelting   refining   aluminium

ALUMINIUM RECYCLING

Aluminium can be recycled. Recycling aluminium is cheaper than making it from bauxite.

USES OF ALUMINIUM

aeroplanes

refrigerators

toothpaste containers

ships

furniture

INTERESTING FACT

Most drink cans are made of aluminium.

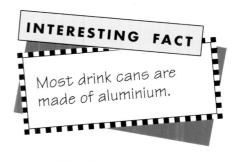
pipes

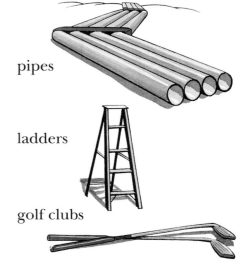
ladders

golf clubs

AMBULANCE

SEE ALSO • Doctor • Drug • Hospital • X-ray

An ambulance is a vehicle which is used to take sick and injured people to hospital. Ambulances have special equipment for treating people.

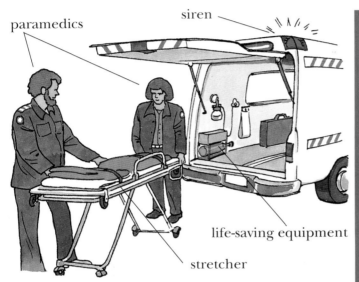

paramedics
siren
life-saving equipment
stretcher

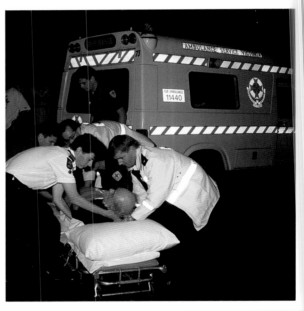

Ambulances in some countries are painted white with red crosses.

Ambulances have a flashing light and a siren. They are switched on to warn traffic that an ambulance is rushing a sick or injured person to hospital.

AIR AMBULANCES ▶

Air ambulances can reach people in difficult places. They provide people with medical care and get them to hospital quickly.

AMPHIBIANS

SEE ALSO
• Animal • Frog
• Vertebrate

Amphibians are a group of cold-blooded animals. They can live in water or on land. An amphibian's body temperature changes with its surroundings.

FROGS AND TOADS

Frogs and toads do not have tails.

strong back legs for jumping

smooth, moist skin

Young frogs are called tadpoles. They live in water and breathe through gills. Adult frogs and toads develop lungs for breathing on land.

NEWTS AND SALAMANDERS

Newts and salamanders have tails.

Newts live in water.

Salamanders live on land.

4 short legs

CAECILIANS

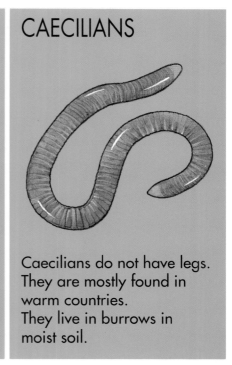

Caecilians do not have legs. They are mostly found in warm countries. They live in burrows in moist soil.

Most amphibians lay their eggs in water in a layer of jelly.

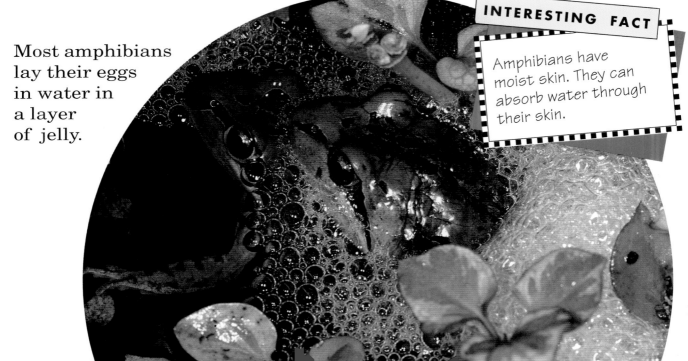

INTERESTING FACT

Amphibians have moist skin. They can absorb water through their skin.

15

ANIMAL

SEE ALSO • Amphibians • Birds • Fish • Insect • Mammal • Reptiles

An animal is a living thing. All animals feed, move and breed. There are over ten million different kinds of animals on Earth.

▲ The giraffe is the tallest animal. Its long neck and long legs allow it to feed from high branches.
Height: 5 metres

All animals can be divided into two groups.

Vertebrates are animals with backbones.

mammals
birds
reptiles
amphibians
fish

Invertebrates are animals without backbones.

single-celled animals
worms
insects
jellyfish
slugs and snails

FOOD

Food provides energy for animals to move. Animals eat food to build and develop their bodies.
• Some animals only eat plants. They are herbivores.
• Some animals only eat other animals. They are carnivores.
• Some animals eat both animals and plants. They are omnivores.

WARM-BLOODED OR COLD-BLOODED?

• A warm-blooded animal's temperature stays the same all the time. Birds and mammals are warm-blooded.
• A cold-blooded animal's temperature changes with its surroundings. Amphibians and reptiles are cold-blooded animals.

INTERESTING FACT

The smallest animals are protozoa. They can only be seen with a microscope.

Different animals have different lifespans. An adult mayfly only lives for a few hours.

The giant tortoise can live for more than 100 years.

Animals use their senses of smell, touch, sight, hearing and taste to find food and protect themselves from enemies.

The elephant is the largest land animal. It uses its trunk for touching and smelling.
Height: 3 metres
Weight: 4 to 5 tonnes

INTERESTING FACT

Chickens used to be wild animals. They lived in forests in South East Asia.

The blue whale is the largest animal on Earth. It can grow up to 30 metres long.

FARM
ANIMALS

People have captured and tamed wild animals. These animals are used to provide milk, meat, skins and wool. Some domestic animals are used for transport.

FERAL
ANIMALS

Feral animals are tamed animals which have escaped and bred in the wild. They often damage the environment and hunt wild animals.

17

ANT

SEE ALSO • Animal • Insect

An ant is a tiny insect. Ants are social insects. Millions of ants live together in large groups called colonies.

PARTS OF A WORKER ANT

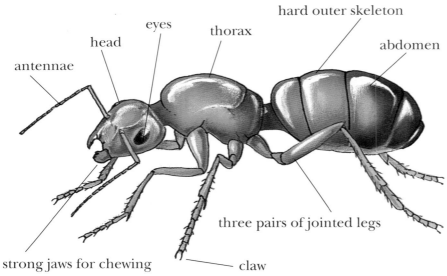

antennae, head, eyes, thorax, hard outer skeleton, abdomen, three pairs of jointed legs, claw, strong jaws for chewing

FOOD

caterpillars

leaves

fungi and other plant and animal material

AN ANT COLONY

Queen:
• spends her whole life laying eggs
• has wings.

Female workers:
• do not lay eggs
• collect food
• look after the nest and care for the young
• do not have wings.

Males:
• mate with the queen
• do not work
• have wings.

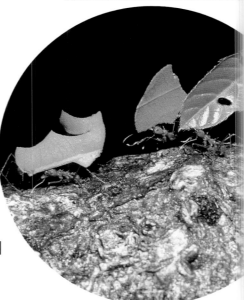

▲ Some ants can lift objects that weigh more than they do.

ANTARCTICA

SEE ALSO
• Arctic • Penguin
• Seal • Whale

Antarctica is the continent around the South Pole. Antarctica is the fifth largest continent in the world and the coldest place on Earth.

ANTARCTICA

Most of the land in Antarctica is covered by a thick sheet of ice.

Most animals live around the coast or in the sea. They have a thick coat of fur or layers of blubber to keep them warm. Only plants such as lichen and moss grow in Antarctica. These low-growing plants are able to survive the cold winds.

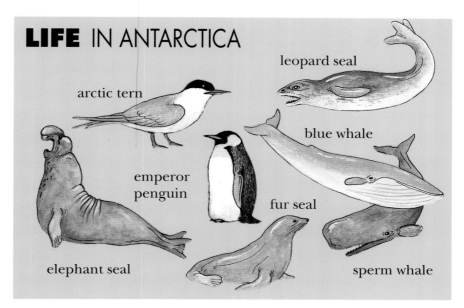

LIFE IN ANTARCTICA

arctic tern

leopard seal

blue whale

emperor penguin

fur seal

elephant seal

sperm whale

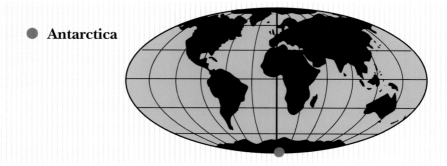

● Antarctica

◀ Scientists make expeditions to Antarctica to explore the land. They study the weather, and animal and plant life.

APE

SEE ALSO • Animal • Mamma
• Monkey

An ape is a mammal. It is the animal most like human beings. Apes have the same bones, muscles and body parts as people.

PARTS OF A CHIMPANZEE

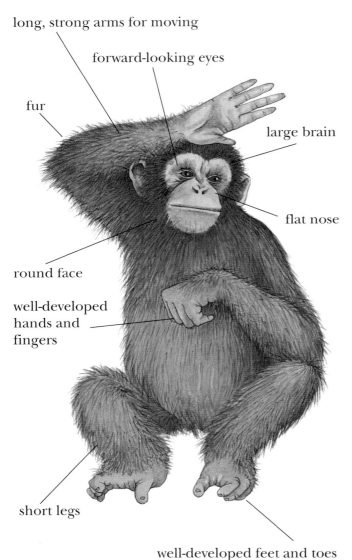

long, strong arms for moving

forward-looking eyes

fur

large brain

flat nose

round face

well-developed hands and fingers

short legs

well-developed feet and toes

Height: 1 to 1.5 metres
Weight: 55 to 80 kilograms

FOOD

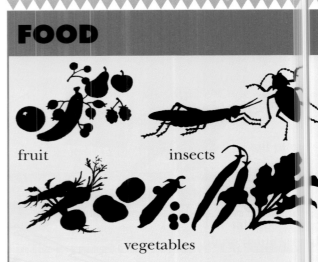

fruit

insects

vegetables

KINDS OF APES
There are four kinds of apes.

Chimpanzees live in groups.

WHERE APES LIVE

- ● **Africa**
  Gorillas and chimpanzees
- ■ **Borneo**
  Orang-utans
- ◆ **South East Asia and East Indies**
  Gibbons

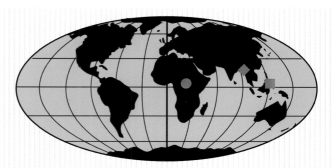

HOW APES LIVE

- Female apes usually give birth to one baby at a time.
- The mother feeds the baby ape for two to three months.
- Young apes usually stay with their mother for a couple of years.

INTERESTING FACT

Chimpanzees are the best tool users after humans.

HOW APES MOVE

Apes can stand upright, but they usually move around on all fours. They can use their arms for moving in trees. They use their hands and feet as we use our hands.

Gorillas live in small groups.

Gibbons live in family groups. They are the smallest apes.

Orang-utans live alone. They live mainly in trees.

ARCHERY

SEE ALSO • Castle

Archery is a sport. You use a bow and arrow, and a target. The bow and arrow is one of the oldest weapons.

◀ HISTORY

Thousands of years ago, people used bows and arrows to hunt for food.

Archers need to stand correctly. The arrow must hit the target. You get points when you hit different colours on the target.

EQUIPMENT

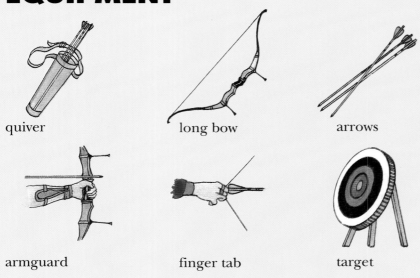

quiver

long bow

arrows

armguard

finger tab

target

ARCTIC

The Arctic is the frozen region around the North Pole. The Arctic Ocean covers the North Pole. It is a frozen ocean.

SEE ALSO
• Antarctica • Seal
• Whale

PLANT LIFE

During the short summer, it is warm enough for small plants to grow in some parts of the Arctic.

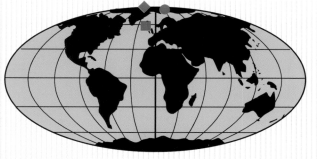

● Arctic Circle
■ Arctic Ocean
◆ North Pole

berries

grasses

mosses

ARCTIC PEOPLE

Lapps and the Inuit are the two main groups of people who live in the Arctic. Since early times, the Inuit have lived in the Arctic.

Many scientists work in the Arctic. ▶

ANIMAL LIFE

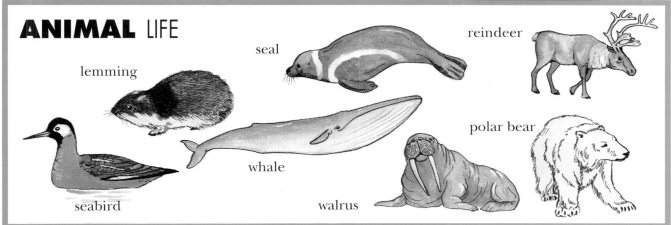

lemming

seal

reindeer

seabird

whale

walrus

polar bear

23

ASTRONAUT

SEE ALSO • Gravity • Moon • Spacecraft • Space Shuttle

An astronaut is a person who is trained to travel in space. Astronauts have to be very fit and healthy. They must spend a long time learning how to live and work in space.

WEIGHTLESSNESS ▶

Astronauts and things float in space because of the lack of gravity.

LIFT-OFF

A spacecraft is rocketed into space.

EATING
IN SPACE

It is difficult to eat or drink in space. Food must be squeezed right into the mouth from packets or it will break up into a haze of crumbs and rubbish. Water must be squeezed from a bottle or sucked through a straw or it will break up into floating droplets.

WORKING
IN SPACE

Astronauts must be able to operate, maintain and repair the spacecraft. They make observations and carry out experiments.

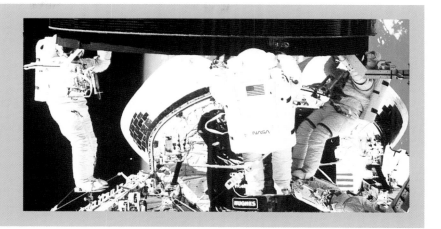

◀ SPLASHDOWN!

Astronauts learn escape and survival skills in case they need to land the spacecraft in an emergency.

INTERESTING FACT

Neil Armstrong was the first person to walk on the Moon, on 20 July 1969.

LIFE SUPPORT SYSTEMS

There is no air in space. Astronauts need life support systems to keep them alive when they are outside the spacecraft. In their backpacks, they have oxygen to breathe and a communication system. Their spacesuits protect them from heat and cold, and harmful radiation.

ASTRONOMY

SEE ALSO
• Meteor • Moon • Satellite
• Star • Telescope • Universe

Astronomy is learning about objects in the Universe. These objects are the Sun, stars, planets, comets and galaxies. Astronomers are scientists who study the Universe.

ASTRONOMY IS AN OLD SCIENCE

People have always tried to learn about the moons, stars and planets in the Universe. Before the invention of the telescope in the seventeenth century, objects in the Universe were too far away for people to see clearly.

OBSERVATORY

Astronomers find out about stars, galaxies and planets from observatories. These are usually built at the top of a mountain so astronomers can have a clear view of the sky. Inside the observatory, they use powerful telescopes.

SATELLITES

Satellites help us to learn more about space. They take photographs of planets such as Neptune. The photographs are transmitted to Earth.

★ ★ ★ ★ ★
STARGAZING

People use special equipment such as telescopes to learn about the Universe. Some people study the stars and planets as a hobby.

INTERESTING FACT

The Sun is a star. During the day the only star you can see is the Sun.

27

ATHLETICS

SEE ALSO • Olympic Games

Athletics are sporting activities. They include running, jumping, throwing and walking events. An athlete is a person who takes part in athletics.

RECORDS ▶
Officials keep time and measure distances so athletes can set records.

Athletics are divided into two kinds: track events and field events.

TRACK EVENTS
Track events include races, sprints, hurdles and relays. Athletes can run long or short distances.

HURDLES
Athletes run and jump over hurdles.

RELAYS
Four-person teams usually race in relays.

FIELD EVENTS

Field events include high jump, long jump, pole vault, discus, javelin, shot-put and hammer throwing.

HAMMER THROWING
The hammer which athletes throw is made of metal.

HIGH JUMP AND POLE VAULT
High jumpers and pole vaulters jump over a crossbar.

SHOT-PUT
A shot-put is a solid metal ball which athletes throw.

JAVELIN
The javelin looks like a spear.

DISCUS
The discus is made of wood or plastic, and has a smooth metal edge.

29

ATMOSPHERE

SEE ALSO
- Air • Earth • Gas
- Weather • Wind

The atmosphere is the layer of air that surrounds the Earth. It contains oxygen that all living things need to breathe. The atmosphere also prevents harmful rays from the Sun reaching the Earth.

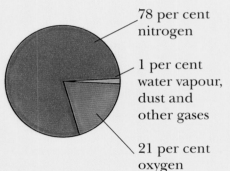

The air we breathe is mostly made of two gases, nitrogen and oxygen, and a mixture of water vapour, dust and small amounts of other gases.

78 per cent nitrogen

1 per cent water vapour, dust and other gases

21 per cent oxygen

INTERESTING FACT

The atmosphere is held in place around the Earth by the pull of the Earth's gravity.

THE ATMOSPHERE HAS FIVE LAYERS

The exosphere is the last layer before outer space. It contains very little air.

The thermosphere is 80 to 480 kilometres above the Earth's surface. The thermosphere is a layer of very thin air.

The mesophere is 50 to 80 kilometres above the Earth's surface.

The stratosphere is 11 to 50 kilometres above the Earth's surface. Jet aircraft fly in this layer to avoid rough weather. The ozone layer is a thin layer within the stratosphere. Ozone is a kind of oxygen gas. It absorbs harmful ultraviolet rays from the Sun.

The troposphere reaches up to 11 kilometres above the ground. It contains most of the air we breathe. Most weather occurs here.

AVALANCHE

• Earthquake • Glacier
• Rain • Skiing

An avalanche is a mass of snow, ice, rocks or earth that becomes loose and slides down the sides of a mountain.

HOW AVALANCHES START

An avalanche can be started by:
- an earth tremor
- heavy winds
- sound vibrations made by skiers
- explosions.

Avalanches can ▲ be dangerous. They can sweep away trees and buildings, and kill people and animals.

People can help to stop avalanches.
- They can plant trees which stop snow sliding down mountains.
- They can build barriers to control snow.
- They can use explosives to stop large amounts of snow from building up.

BALLET

SEE ALSO
• Dancing • Drama
• Music • Orchestra

Ballet uses dance, music and mime to tell a story.
It is usually performed in a theatre.

TRAINING AND PRACTICE

A choreographer plans dance movements and teaches them to the ballet dancers.

A BALLET PERFORMANCE

Music, scenery, costumes and lighting are an important part of the ballet.

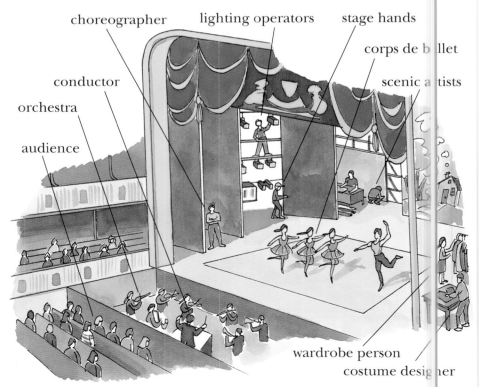

choreographer

lighting operators

stage hands

corps de ballet

scenic artists

conductor

orchestra

audience

wardrobe person

costume designer

FEET POSITIONS

There are five feet positions.
Every ballet movement begins and ends with
one of these positions.

first position second position third position fourth position fifth position

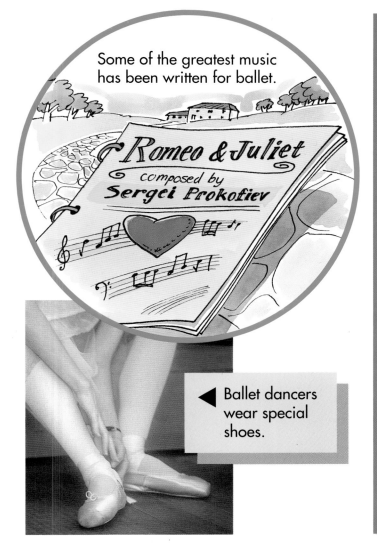

Some of the greatest music
has been written for ballet.

Romeo & Juliet composed by Sergei Prokofiev

◀ Ballet dancers
wear special
shoes.

SEVEN MOVEMENTS

Seven dance movements
are used in ballet. Some
are shown here.

A *plié* is a bending
movement.

This *arabesque*
uses a bending
movement.

A *pas-de-chat*
uses darting
and jumping.

A *pirouette* is a
turning step.

A *glissade* is
a sliding
movement.

BALLOON

SEE ALSO • Air • Gas • Transport • Weather

A balloon is an airtight bag filled with light gases. It can rise in the air. A balloon floats in the air like a cork floats in water.

HOW HOT-AIR BALLOONS WORK

1. When air becomes warm, it becomes lighter. In a hot-air balloon, the air inside the balloon is heated by burning gas.

2. When the air inside the balloon is lighter than the air outside, the balloon rises.

3. To return to the ground, small amounts of gas are released through the valve.

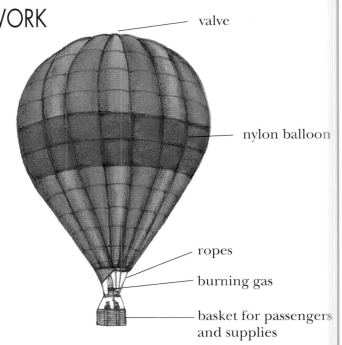

valve

nylon balloon

ropes

burning gas

basket for passengers and supplies

There are different types of balloons.
• Party balloons.
• Hot-air balloons.

◀ HISTORY

The first hot-air balloon was flown in 1783.

INTERESTING FACT

Hot-air balloons were used for spying during the First and Second World Wars.

HOW BALLOONS ARE USED ▶

Weather balloons carry instruments which record changes in the atmosphere.
The information is sent back to weather stations. It is used to forecast the weather.

Balloonists fly in hot-air balloons for pleasure. Ballooning is a sport. ▼

BANK

SEE ALSO
• Money

A bank is a place where people deposit their money. People and businesses use banks. They can use cheques and bankcards to pay their bills and to buy things. Banks also lend money.

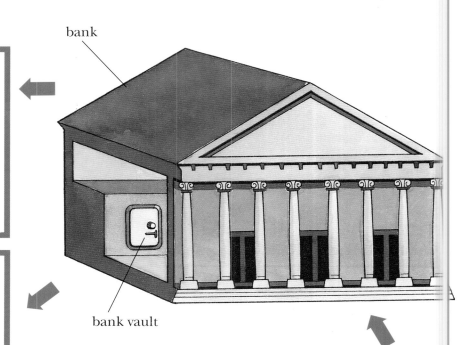

bank

bank vault

Banks lend money to:
- governments
- businesses
- farmers
- factories
- shops
- people who want to buy houses, cars and other things.

People who want to borrow money from banks are called borrowers. They pay back the money they borrow, plus interest. Interest is a fee people pay for borrowing money.

People who deposit savings and wages in a bank are called depositors. Depositors earn interest. The interest is a fee banks pay for using depositors' money.

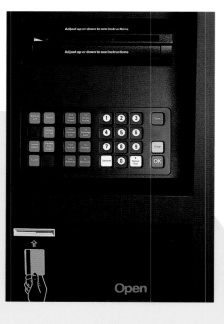

AUTOMATED TELLER MACHINE

Automated teller machines help bank customers withdraw and deposit money at any time.

BASEBALL

SEE ALSO
• Cricket • Tennis

Baseball is a field game. Two teams are needed to play. Each team has nine players. One team bats while the other team fields.

SCORING

One team must score more runs than the other team when it is batting. The batter must go from the batting position to home plate to score one run. The batter can stop at any base.

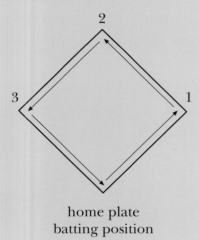

home plate
batting position

Baseball is ▶ played on a large diamond-shaped field.

EQUIPMENT

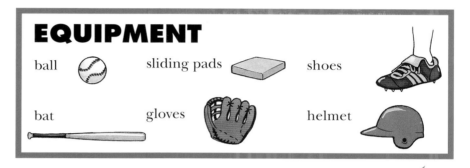

ball   sliding pads   shoes

bat   gloves   helmet

BATTING

The batter hits the ball as far as he can. The catcher stands behind the batter. The catcher is protected by a mask, chest protector and a padded mitt.

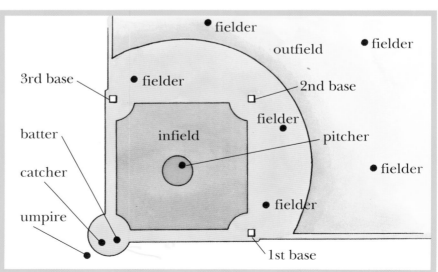

fielder
outfield
fielder
3rd base
fielder
2nd base
fielder
batter
infield
pitcher
catcher
fielder
umpire
fielder
1st base

BASKETBALL

SEE ALSO
• Netball

Basketball is a game played with a large ball. It is played with two teams of five players. Basketball can be played indoors or outdoors.

SCORING

Each team tries to win points by shooting a basketball into a basketball goal at each end of the court.

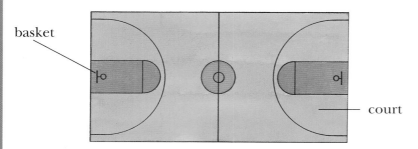

basket

court

A basketball court is 29 metres long and 15 metres wide.

HOW TO PLAY

The ball may be passed, dribbled or bounced along the floor by a single player.

EQUIPMENT

a basketball

two baskets fastened to backboards, which are the goals

KINDS OF BASKETBALL

Players can play in wheelchairs. Deaf (hearing-impaired) players can use hand signals. Visually-impaired players use a basketball with a bell inside.

BAT

SEE ALSO
• Animal • Mammal
• Radar • Vertebrate

A bat is a small, furry animal.
It is the only mammal that can fly.
A bat's wings are sheets of skin on the sides of its body.

PARTS OF A RED BAT

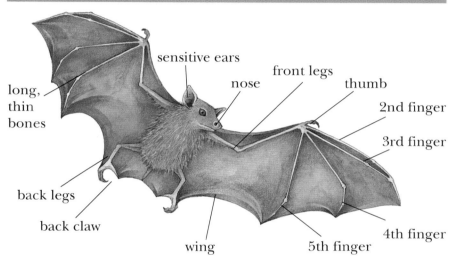

sensitive ears
front legs
nose
thumb
long, thin bones
2nd finger
3rd finger
back legs
back claw
4th finger
wing
5th finger

Length: 11.5 centimetres

FOOD

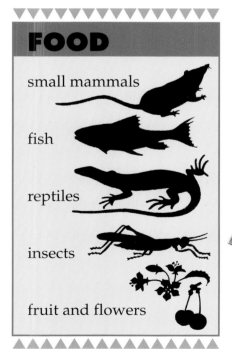

small mammals

fish

reptiles

insects

fruit and flowers

HOW BATS LIVE

• Female bats give birth to one or two young each year.
• Most bats spend the day sleeping upside down. Bats hunt for food at night.

WHERE BATS LIVE

Bats are found all over the world except in the Arctic and the Antarctic.

Fruit bats are called flying foxes.

BEAR

SEE ALSO
• Animal • Koala
• Mammal • Panda

A bear is a mammal. It is a large, strong animal covered with thick fur. Bears usually live alone. They can be fierce fighters when protecting their young.

PARTS OF A BROWN BEAR

small round ears

broad head

poor eyesight

keen sense of smell

strong jaws

thick fur

strong, short legs

big strong paws for digging and holding food, and defending itself against enemies

Average weight: 750 kilograms
Average height: 2 metres

KINDS OF BEAR

There are seven different kinds of bears.

Polar bear

Sloth bear

Sun bear

Brown bear – Alaskan brown bear and grizzly brown bear

Black bear – American black bear and Asiatic black bear

Spectacled bear

Panda bear

HOW BEARS LIVE

• Bears usually live alone. They walk a long way to hunt for food.
• During winter, bears sleep in their dens. They live off their body fat until spring.
• Female bears give birth to one to four cubs in winter.
• Bears stay with their mothers for one to two years until they can hunt for food themselves.

WHERE BEARS LIVE

● North America
■ South America
◆ Greenland
★ Asia

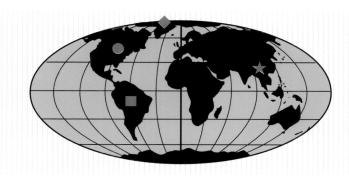

HOW BEARS MOVE

Bears are slow-moving animals. Some bears can climb trees. Many bears are strong swimmers.

FOOD

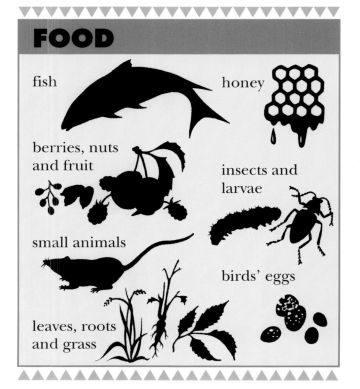

fish

honey

berries, nuts and fruit

insects and larvae

small animals

birds' eggs

leaves, roots and grass

BEE

SEE ALSO
• Animal • Flower • Insect
• Life Cycle

A bee is an insect. Bees collect nectar and pollen from flowers. This is made into honey and stored in hives for food. There are 20 000 kinds of bees.

PARTS OF A BEE

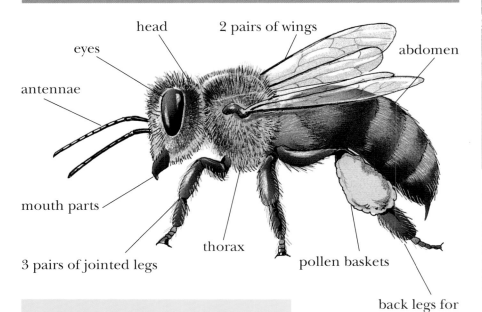

- head
- 2 pairs of wings
- eyes
- abdomen
- antennae
- mouth parts
- 3 pairs of jointed legs
- thorax
- pollen baskets
- back legs for self-defence

Bees collect nectar and pollen from flowers. The nectar is made into honey. As bees collect nectar and pollen, they fertilize crops and flowers.

BEE-KEEPING

Farmers keep bees to collect honey and beeswax. Bee-keeping can also be a hobby for some people.

INTERESTING FACT

A bee must visit over 4000 flowers to collect enough nectar to make one tablespoon of honey.

WHERE BEES LIVE

Bees live in most parts of the world, except the Arctic and the Antarctic.

KINDS OF BEES

There are many kinds of bees. Some are solitary bees. They live alone. Some bees such as bumblebees and honeybees are social bees. They live in large groups called colonies.

A HONEYBEE COLONY

A honeybee colony has thousands of workers, a few hundred drones and one queen.

Queen bee:
• spends all her life laying eggs.

Drone bees (male bees):
• do not have a sting
• mate with the queen.

Worker bees:
• collect nectar and pollen from flowers
• care for young
• clean and guard the hive.

INSIDE A HONEYBEE HIVE

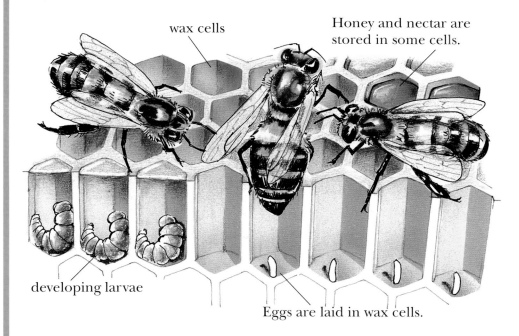

wax cells

Honey and nectar are stored in some cells.

developing larvae

Eggs are laid in wax cells.

LIFE CYCLE OF A HONEYBEE

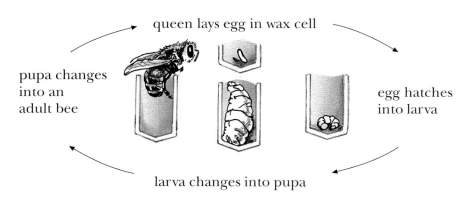

queen lays egg in wax cell

pupa changes into an adult bee

egg hatches into larva

larva changes into pupa

43

BEETLE

SEE ALSO • Animal • Insect • Life Cycle

A beetle is an insect. Beetles are one of the largest groups of insects. They live in most parts of the world. Beetles come in all shapes, sizes and colours.

PARTS OF AN ADULT BEETLE

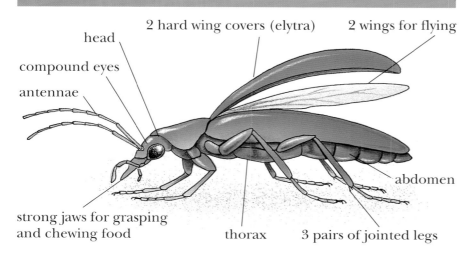

head
2 hard wing covers (elytra)
2 wings for flying
compound eyes
antennae
strong jaws for grasping and chewing food
thorax
3 pairs of jointed legs
abdomen

WHERE BEETLES LIVE

- in water
- on top of the ground
- under the ground
- on other animals

A water beetle can swim well.

FOOD

Beetles feed on plants, and dead plant and animal matter.

USEFUL BEETLES

- Ladybirds feed on other insects which damage plants.
- The dung beetle clears away dung and dead animals.

LIFE CYCLE OF A BEETLE

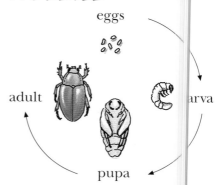

eggs
adult
larva
pupa

44

BELL

SEE ALSO • Music • Newspaper

A bell can make a clear, musical sound. It is a hollow cup-shaped object with a clapper inside. When the bell is moved, the clapper touches the sides and chimes.

HISTORY

Hundreds of years ago, town criers rang bells to attract attention as they read out important notices.

CARILLONS

A carillon is a large set of bells that are hung together. Teams of ringers ring the bells in sequence. Some bells are pulled by ropes. Others are operated by electricity.

FAMOUS BELL

The Liberty Bell is in the USA. It was rung to announce the signing of the Declaration of Independence in 1776.

Hand bells ▼ can be rung to make music.

BICYCLE

SEE ALSO
• Motor Cycle • Pollution
• Transport

A bicycle is a vehicle which has two wheels. One wheel is behind the other on a metal frame. The rider balances on a seat and pushes the pedals to move. The rider uses the handlebars to steer the bicycle.

PARTS OF A BICYCLE

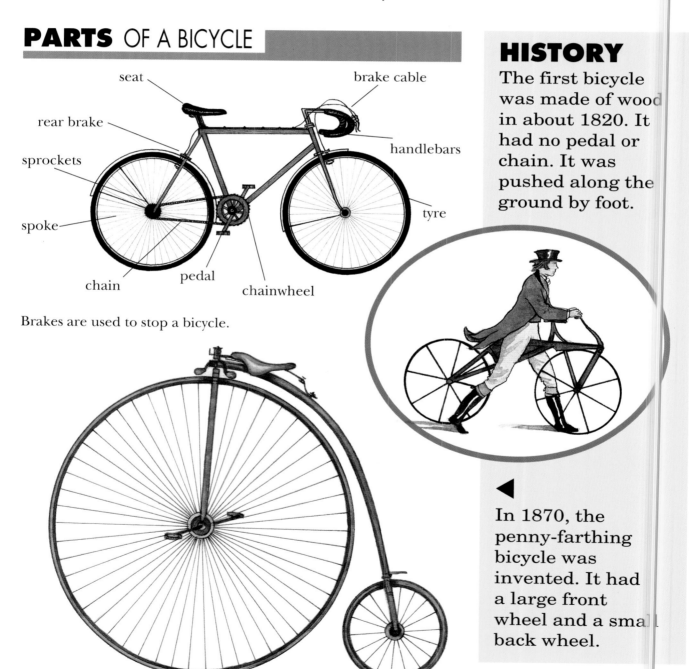

seat

brake cable

rear brake

handlebars

sprockets

spoke

tyre

chain

pedal

chainwheel

Brakes are used to stop a bicycle.

HISTORY

The first bicycle was made of wood in about 1820. It had no pedal or chain. It was pushed along the ground by foot.

◄

In 1870, the penny-farthing bicycle was invented. It had a large front wheel and a small back wheel.

HOW A BICYCLE WORKS

1. The rider pushes the pedals.
2. The chainwheel goes around.
3. The chain is pulled around and turns the sprocket.
4. The back wheel is turned by the sprocket.

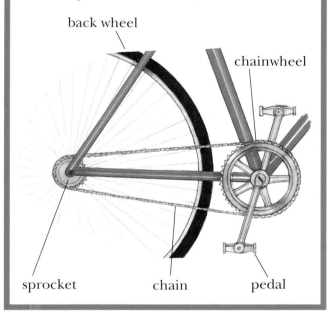

back wheel

chainwheel

sprocket   chain   pedal

TRANSPORT

Many people travel around cities and towns by bicycle. Bicycles are a quiet and clean mode of transport.

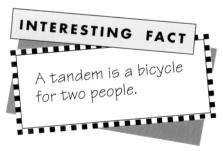

INTERESTING FACT

A tandem is a bicycle for two people.

◀ SPORT

People use bicycles for exercise and sport.

BIRD

SEE ALSO • Animal • Vertebrate

A bird is an animal with feathers.
All birds have wings, but some birds cannot fly.

PARTS OF A BIRD

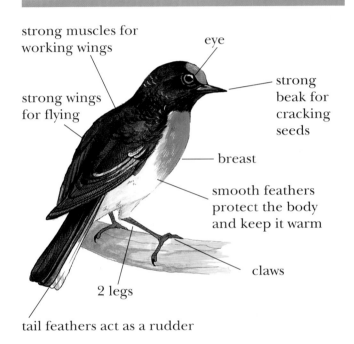

strong muscles for working wings

eye

strong wings for flying

strong beak for cracking seeds

breast

smooth feathers protect the body and keep it warm

claws

2 legs

tail feathers act as a rudder

FOOD

seeds

insects

fruit

snakes and lizard

fish

rats and mice

birds

honey

HOW BIRDS LIVE

• Birds lay eggs with hard shell .
• The young develop inside the egg, feeding on the yolk.
• After a few weeks, the eggs hatch. The young birds, nestling , have no feathers and cannot see.
• Usually young birds stay in th nest where they are fed and protected by the parent birds.
• The young birds leave the nest when they are big enough to fly and find their own food.

BEAKS

Birds use their beaks to find food, to gather material to build nests and to preen themselves. Birds' beaks are suited to finding different kinds of food.

beaks for cracking seed

beaks for straining water and mud

beaks for spearing and cracking food

beaks for killing and tearing food

beaks for chiselling and cutting holes in trees

beaks for probing to find nectar and tiny insects

FEET

A bird's feet tell you where it lives.

feet for wading in ponds and streams

feet for swimming and paddling in water

feet with four curved claws for climbing

feet for clamping on to branches

feet for grasping, catching and killing prey

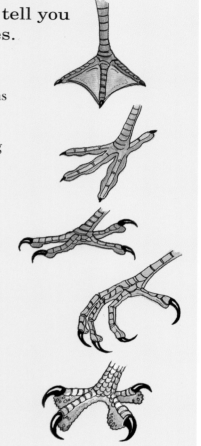

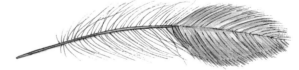

FEATHERS

- Feathers protect birds and keep them warm.
- Feathers fit together to make a smooth surface for flying.
- Feathers can act as camouflage.
- Some birds use their feathers to find a mate.
- Coloured feathers can help a flock of birds keep together.

SIZE OF BIRDS

Birds vary in size.
- The smallest bird is the hummingbird. It is five centimetres long.
- The largest bird is the ostrich. It is 2.5 metres tall. The ostrich cannot fly.

◀ MIGRATION

Many birds travel long distances. They migrate to find food, a place to breed or a warmer place in which to live. Some birds spend summer in one place and fly to another place in winter.

BIRDWATCHING

People watch birds for a hobby. Scientists watch birds to learn about the environment. They use binoculars to see the birds clearly.

BIRD SONGS

Birds sing to attract mates. They also warn other birds to stay out of their territory.

BIRD CALLS

Birds communicate with each other using bird calls. Bird calls can warn of danger and keep birds in a flock together. Birds also call to each other when they find food.

EXTINCT BIRDS

Some birds no longer exist. They have become extinct. The dodo became extinct in the seventeenth century.

BIRDS OF THE WORLD

eastern rosella

yellow bellied sapsucker

paradise flycatcher

eagle

hummingbird

barn owl

stork

crested penguin

crowned crane

toucan

golden oricle

great blue
touraco

puffin

dipper

mandarin duck

BLOOD

SEE ALSO • Heart • Human Body • Lungs

Blood is the red fluid in the body. The heart pumps blood around the body. Blood carries oxygen from the lungs to every part of the body. Blood carries carbon dioxide back to the lungs.

HOW BLOOD WORKS

Blood contains a liquid called plasma.
Plasma contains white cells, red cells and platelets.

White cells fight disease and infection.

Red cells carry oxygen around your body.

Platelets help blood to clot and stop wounds bleeding.

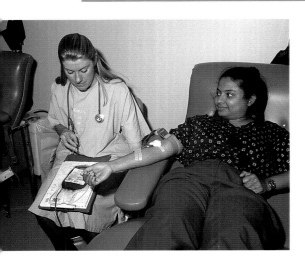

◄ BLOOD DONORS

Blood donors give blood to a blood bank. Their blood is stored. It is given to people in accidents and in operations. The donor's body soon makes up more blood.

When a person falls over, the platelets ▶ in their blood clot quickly. The platelets make a scab over the wound.

BOAT

SEE ALSO
• Canoe • Hovercraft • Ship
• Submarine • Yacht

A boat is a small vessel that can move on water.
Boats are usually smaller than ships.
They travel on rivers, canals, lakes and along coasts.

HISTORY

People have used boats for
thousands of years.
• Boats have been used to
carry people across streams
and along rivers.
• Boats have been used
for fishing.
• Boats have been used for
trading and exploring.

In the 1800s, steam, propellers
and paddles were used to move
boats. Before then, sails, oars
and poles were used to
move boats.

KINDS OF BOATS

People use boats for sport, leisure
and work.

motor boats

fishing boats

canoes

rowing boats

tugboats

houseboats

sailing boats

SAILING SHIPS ▶

Sailing ships have a lot of sails to catch the
wind. This moves the ship. Hundreds of years
ago, explorers used sailing ships to travel long
distances to places where they had not been before.

BOOK

SEE ALSO • Library • Newspaper • Paper • Printing

A book is made up of sheets of paper called pages. The pages are bound together at one end. Words and pictures are printed on the pages of a book. Books have a cover on the front and back to protect the pages.

KINDS OF BOOKS

Fiction books include poetry, drama, fairy tales, nursery rhymes, mystery, adventure stories and lots more.

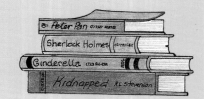

Factual books contain information.

- Dictionaries contain information about words.

- Atlases contain information about countries and places.

- Encyclopedias contain information about many different subjects. The entries are arranged alphabetically.

HISTORY OF BOOKS

1. Long ago people scratched symbols on walls of caves and pyramids.

2. A kind of paper made from a reed was used by the Greeks, Egyptians and Romans.

3. The first real paper was invented in China about 2000 years ago.

4. The first books were called manuscripts. Monks wrote manuscripts by hand.

PEOPLE WHO HELP MAKE BOOKS

author

illustrator

editor

In 1438, Johannes Gutenberg invented the printing machine in Germany. Lots of copies of books could be printed at the same time.

designer

printer

storeperson

BRAIN

SEE ALSO • Ears • Eye • Human Body • Nose • Skin • Taste

The brain controls everything the body does. The brain enables us to move, think, learn, imagine, dream and remember. The brain is the most important part of the nervous system.

PARTS OF THE BRAIN

Cerebrum:
- controls the left and right sides of the body
- controls hearing, smell and taste
- controls sight
- controls touch.

This part of the brain affects consciousness, creativity and personality.

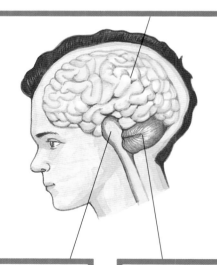

Medulla:
- controls breathing, heartbeat and digestion.

Cerebellum:
- controls the muscles that help us to move
- controls balance and coordination.

The brain sends and receives messages to and from other parts of the body. The messages travel along nerves between the brain and the body. Nerves send messages from the tongue, eyes, nose, ears and skin to the brain.

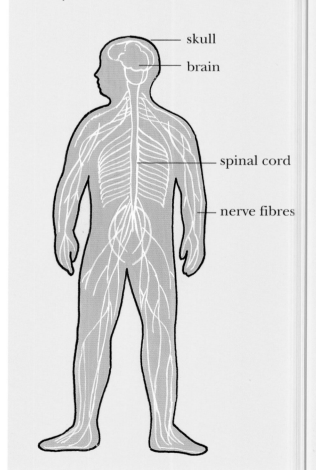

skull

brain

spinal cord

nerve fibres

The brain is soft, greyish pink and wrinkled. It is protected inside the head by the skull.

THE SENSES

Different parts of the brain control sight, hearing, touch, taste and smell. We use our senses all the time to do many different things.

INTERESTING FACT

Your brain has learned to move your eyes from left to right as you read. Some languages read from top to bottom, or from right to left. The brain has to learn to move the eyes in a different way.

BREAD

SEE ALSO
• Farming • Food • Grass
• Shop

Bread is a food. It is eaten by people all over the world. People have always made bread. It is made from grain. Different kinds of grain make different bread. Bread is a very healthy food.

WHEAT GROWING

Rye, wheat, rice, barley, corn and oats are all grains that are used to make bread.

Bread can have many different colours and tastes. To make brown bread, the whole grain is used. To make white bread, only the inside of the grain is used. Flat breads do not have yeast.

KINDS OF BREAD

French baguette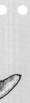

Greek bread

flat Lebanese bread

pumpernickel

brown bread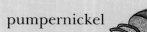

white sliced bread

fruit bread

bread rolls

flat Swedish bread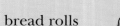

HOW BREAD IS MADE

1. Grain is grown.

2. Grain is ground into flour.

3. Flour is mixed with yeast, salt and water.

4. Dough is left so that the yeast can ferment. This makes the dough rise.

5. Dough is kneaded.

6. The dough is put into tins and baked.

7. The bread is packaged and sent to shops.

BRICKS

SEE ALSO • Bridge • Castle • House

Bricks are used for building. A brick is block shaped.
It is made of crushed clay which is mixed with water.
Bricks are baked in ovens or kilns to make them hard.

BUILDING A WALL

The bricks are laid down flat so
they overlap in rows. They are
then bound together with mortar.
Mortar is a soft paste made from
cement, sand, lime and water.

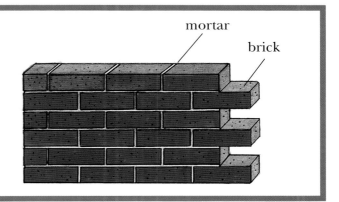

mortar

brick

BRICKLAYING ▼

A bricklayer is a person
who lays bricks to make
something. Bricklayers
use a trowel to apply
the mortar.

HISTORY

The ancient Egyptians made bricks and tiles
using clay from the Nile River. They mixed the
clay with straw. The bricks were left outside
to harden.

BRIDGE

SEE ALSO • Bricks • Road • Transport • Water

A bridge is a large structure that is built over water or across land. Bridges make it possible for people, cars and trains to cross rivers, valleys and other obstacles.

HISTORY

The first bridges were made by placing trees or rocks over obstacles.

KINDS OF BRIDGES

There are four kinds of bridges.

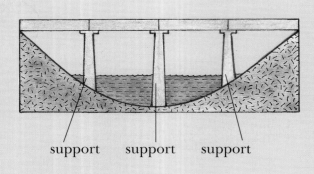

support   support   support

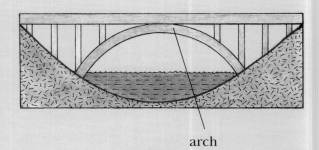

arch

Beam bridge
A beam bridge is supported by columns underneath. More supports can make a beam bridge longer.

Arch bridge
The shape of the arch supports the bridge.

AN AQUEDUCT ▶

An aqueduct looks like a bridge. It carries water across a valley.

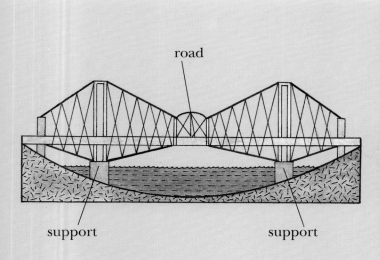

road

support

support

Cantilever bridge

A cantilever bridge is usually built in two sections. Each end supports itself and the two sections meet in the middle.

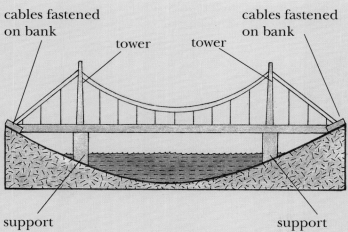

cables fastened on bank

tower

tower

cables fastened on bank

support

support

Suspension bridge

The weight of the bridge rests on the two towers which carry the suspension cables supporting the bridge.

BUTTERFLIES AND MOTHS

SEE ALSO
• Animal • Insect
• Life Cycle

Butterflies and moths are insects. They belong to the same group of insects. Butterflies and moths have four wings which are covered with scales.

PARTS OF A BUTTERFLY

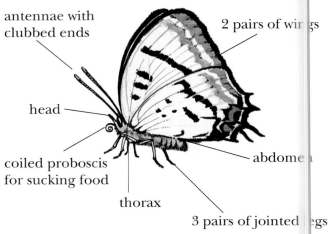

antennae with clubbed ends

2 pairs of wings

head

coiled proboscis for sucking food

abdomen

thorax

3 pairs of jointed legs

LIFE CYCLE OF A BUTTERFLY

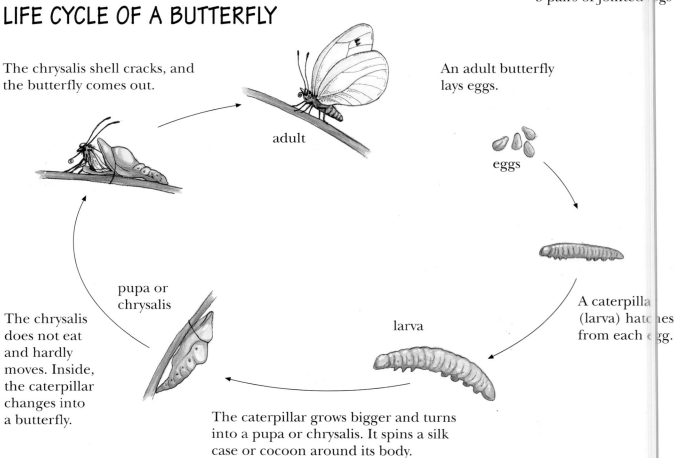

The chrysalis shell cracks, and the butterfly comes out.

adult

An adult butterfly lays eggs.

eggs

pupa or chrysalis

The chrysalis does not eat and hardly moves. Inside, the caterpillar changes into a butterfly.

larva

A caterpillar (larva) hatches from each egg.

The caterpillar grows bigger and turns into a pupa or chrysalis. It spins a silk case or cocoon around its body.

BUTTERFLIES AND MOTHS

BUTTERFLY LARVA

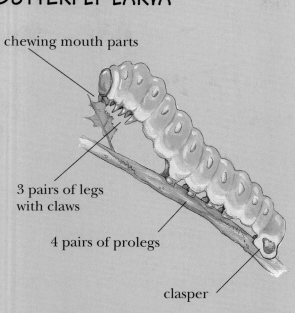

chewing mouth parts

3 pairs of legs with claws

4 pairs of prolegs

clasper

Caterpillars are the larvae in the life cycle of the butterfly. They feed on plants. They have four pairs of fleshy prolegs and three pairs of legs with claws. Caterpillars are food for other insects and birds.

BUTTERFLIES AND MOTHS

- Butterflies usually hold their wings up when resting. Moths hold their wings flat.
- Butterflies fly during the day. Moths usually fly at night.
- Butterflies have antennae with clubs on the end. Moths have feathery antennae.
- Butterflies pollinate flowers.

SIZE OF BUTTERFLIES

There are about 15 000 different kinds of butterflies. The largest butterflies have a wingspan of 30 centimetres. The smallest butterflies have a wingspan of 12 millimetres.

BUTTERFLIES AROUND THE WORLD

broad bordered acraea

large striped swordtail

regent skipper

yellow spot jewel

common pearl
white butterfly

Ulysses

chequered swallowtail

common
grass yellow
butterfly

blue triangle

Cape York birdwing

swallowtail